Paul Harris

Improve your teaching!

Teaching beginners

A new approach for instrumental and singing teachers

The companion book to *Improve your teaching!*

FABER *ff* MUSIC

© 2008 by Faber Music Ltd
This edition first published in 2008
3 Queen Square London WC1N 3AU
Music processed by Jeanne Roberts
Design by Susan Clarke
Printed in England by Caligraving Ltd

ISBN10: 0-571-53175-X
EAN13: 978-0-571-53175-2

To buy Faber Music publications or to find out about the full range of titles
available please contact your local music retailer or Faber Music sales enquiries:
Faber Music Ltd, Burnt Mill, Elizabeth Way, Harlow CM20 2HX
Tel: +44 (0) 1279 82 89 82   Fax: +44 (0) 1279 82 89 83
sales@fabermusic.com   fabermusic.com

UK/USA terminology		
bar	=	measure
crotchet	=	quarter note
minim	=	half note
quaver	=	eighth note
semibreve	=	whole note

Contents

Foreword

Paul Harris, as teacher and writer, always asks perceptive questions which revise and refine our view of what it takes to be a good teacher. In his last book, *Improve your teaching!*, Paul proposes a way forward that he terms 'Simultaneous Learning', where both the student and teacher perceive that the lesson is a journey that involves two (or more) people imaginatively investigating the ways of technical, musical and human insight. The benefits are likely to be manifold. Not least, the teacher's own sense of pride in their privileged position percolates through to their students and the learning experience is lifted onto a new plane of potential accomplishment and meaning.

This principle also lies at the core of *Teaching Beginners* and perhaps requires an even greater sense of self-awareness from the teacher of what it really feels like to be a beginner and how fine are the lines between perceived success and failure by the pupil. How many profoundly musical people have unnecessarily lost confidence in their ability to learn to play or sing because of unmotivated and unimaginative teaching in the first few weeks?

This book openly challenges teachers in the way Paul Harris has challenged himself, constructively analysing the satisfaction to be had in trying out new ideas to instil both pleasure and achievement in learning at the most formative stage. Paul's approach gives teachers and pupils' proper 'confidence tricks' (in the best sense), which build self-assurance and develop a vocabulary of discovery.

I know a lot of people find the prospect of teaching people from scratch about as enticing as climbing Everest without oxygen or boots. I for one now feel compelled to try it as a profoundly vibrant activity. Not least, one is reminded that if we were not to recognise the special challenges of this seminal part of musical life – passing on the benefits of our musical experience to brave beginners (in the most thought-provoking and responsible way possible) – the future would indeed be bleak. As an educator, *par excellence*, Paul Harris has no intention of letting that happen. Quite the opposite. Under his guidance, the currency of teaching is justly elevated.

Professor Jonathan Freeman-Attwood
Principal, Royal Academy of Music

The way in ...

❝ The real voyage of discovery consists not in seeking new lands,
but in seeing with new eyes. ❞
Marcel Proust

A colleague once said to me that teaching beginners was real drudgery. How wrong he was. Teaching beginners is certainly a huge challenge; it is also a huge responsibility, but one that reaps enormous rewards. Above all it is a real joy.

The way we learn to play a musical instrument has changed very much over the last hundred years or so. Look at an old orchestral instrumental tutor and you will notice that by the bottom of the first page beginners were expected (somehow) to have instantaneously absorbed quite advanced rhythmic and technical skills! Things were a little different in piano tutors – young ladies were expected to play the piano as part of their social education, so learning methods were geared more to the younger beginner – but they weren't much fun. Today we have a host of colourful tutors to choose from – but none of these tells us much about how to teach beginners. It is very much a hit-and-miss affair.

I was very lucky with my first instrumental teacher. He was inspiring and fun and certainly the reason why I became a musician. Perhaps the same is true for you. Those first few lessons are crucial to the way a young musician will develop.

This book looks at all the issues concerning the teaching of beginners. And by beginners I mean the average beginner. One of my pupils (who was already a good reader) came back at the end of the second week's practice having polished off an entire tutor book. This is unusual! All pupils will move forward at their own particular pace – but whether they are, on the surface, slow or fast learners, whether they come with or without previous musical experience, all the suggestions made in this book can be applied. In general the strategies introduced in the four 'stages' (discussed in chapters two to five) will probably fill the first term. But it may fill more or less time. It doesn't matter. Go at your own pace and that of your pupils.

There are many ideas and strategies in this book. Don't feel that you have to absorb them all. Just pick and choose those which you think would be most helpful to your teaching. Some of the ideas in the following pages will challenge, some will affirm, but whichever, I hope you will emerge energised and full of (renewed) enthusiasm for your teaching.

Having a reasonable working knowledge of the Simultaneous Learning process, as outlined in *Improve Your Teaching!*, would be helpful but is not in any way vital.

I would like to thank many friends and pupils who continually reinforce my love of teaching and the teaching process. Particularly among them I want to say a special thanks to Robert Tucker for constantly challenging my ideas; Tony Meredith who has read the manuscript with a fine toothcomb; Brian Ley for bringing his great experience to bear; Professor John Davies for questioning virtually every word and Sally Adams, Rupert Burchett, Richard Crozier, Jean Cockburn, Jeannette Holder, Graeme Humphrey, Diana Jackson, Christopher Swann, Alan Taylor, Hector Wells, and members of the Hallé Orchestra and Northern Sinfonia for many very helpful suggestions. Finally, all at Faber Music, especially Lesley Rutherford, Richard King and Kathryn Knight for their constant encouragement and support.

> *Pleasure is the state of being*
> *brought about by what you learn.*
> *Learning is the process of*
> *entering into the experience of this*
> *kind of pleasure.*
> *No pleasure, no learning.*
> *No learning, no pleasure.*
> Wang Ken, *Song of Joy*

1 Entering our world

The beginning is in the end

What do you teach pupils in their very first lesson? Spend a few moments and make a mental note of the kind of thing you usually do. Are there any principles that you follow? Do you like to begin work on your favourite tutor book right away? Or do you save it up for a lesson or two and establish some basic concepts? Do you teach your pupils how the instrument works? Do you begin to teach notation straightaway? Do you engage your pupils in creative activity?

Let's jump ahead twelve years or so to consider outstanding music students on the point of graduating from a music conservatoire. What, in general, would you expect of them? Again spend a few moments and make a mental note of your thoughts.

Let's deal with the graduating students first. They will:
• have an immaculate technique
• play with a highly developed sense of rhythm
• have a sophisticated control of sound
• instill their performances with deeply-felt musical meaning.

An immaculate technique is linked with an advanced control of all the appropriate muscles, which in turn is related directly to a tension-free posture (and tension-free thoughts). A highly-developed sense of rhythm is a consequence of a reliable and instinctive sense of pulse. A wonderful sound results from listening with a well-tutored and discerning musical ear together with a profound concern for tone quality. And performances of deep musical meaning result from a well-developed imagination (plus that special something we might call ingredient 'X').

Can you identify the embryo of those students in your pupils coming in for their first lesson? Is there a set of principles that rings true for both ends of the teaching spectrum? Can you see how the qualities in the four bullet points above might be introduced in that very first lesson? Spend a few moments considering these questions.

We can start to set up a tension-free posture from the moment our pupils first sit at the piano or take hold of their instrument. We can lay the foundation of rhythm by introducing the idea of a steady pulse. We can instill a care and concern for sound from their very first attempts (even if the actual quality may fall somewhat short!) and we can encourage pupils to inject simple meaning into whatever they play. Some principles seem to be emerging ...

The Four Ps

There is indeed a set of four underlying principles that provide a connecting thread through every lesson a developing musician receives, from lesson one onwards. They will form the foundation of our teaching and subsequently create drive and momentum ensuring that every pupil is really given the potential for musical fulfilment, whether he or she wishes to end up a concert soloist, a pop singer or just wants to be able to play a few tunes for pleasure. They are:

Posture
Pulse
Phonology
Personality

Posture

Setting up good posture will guarantee that our pupils have the best chance to develop that immaculate technique. From good posture comes good technique. So straightaway take great care to establish the correct sitting or standing position. The correct use and control of all muscles and muscular processes when holding the instrument or sitting at the piano will reap enormous rewards. Monitor and praise good posture, regularly.

Pulse

Developing a real awareness and control of pulse is of inestimable value. It will ensure the ability to 'play in time' and understand note lengths. It will help pupils to nurture that sense of rhythm and indeed all things rhythmical which will give a performance real vitality, shape and movement at all levels.

Phonology

This impressive word comes from the ancient Greek 'phone' meaning 'sound'. We want our pupils to *care* about the sound they make. It may not be very sophisticated (indeed it may be truly awful to our ears in the early stages!) but we want to stimulate pupils' awareness so that they are always striving to make the best possible sound. Even in lesson one! When sound resonates, when it has quality, it becomes evocative and communicative. And, of course, a concern for sound and for learning to listen to it musically and intelligently will connect with all things we understand as 'aural'.

Personality

What is the difference between noise and music? That's a big (philosophical) question! But for the sake of simplicity and brevity let's say the answer is in *the intention behind the noise*. If we play a note loudly it's merely a loud note.

But if we play it loudly with the intention of conveying 'anger' or 'triumph', it becomes a musical statement. The sound is filled with musical personality. Noise is transformed into music. From the very start we can teach our pupils that music is a way of expressing something. It is the way into filling our pupils' performances with musical character.

Watch your language!

We don't of course need to introduce any of these principles by using the labels above. Depending on the age and experience of the pupil, there are all sorts of possible ways to simplify each principle. For a particularly young pupil we might say:

- *First we're going to learn how to stand/sit properly and hold our instrument.*
- *You have a heartbeat that keeps you going – we're going to learn about music's heartbeat that keeps it going.*
- *Let's begin to hear what a wonderful sound you can make on your instrument.*
- *Whenever we make a musical sound, it means something. A loud sound might say 'Wake up!' or a soft sound might say 'go to sleep ...'. Musical sounds can paint a picture or tell a story.*

The fifth P

There is in fact a fifth P, though it is not another principle. It is, however, important and concerns the *practicalities* of the instrument. Some instruments will need careful assembling; all will need looking after. It is important to spend some time on this fifth P in the first lesson, but try to deal with it quickly and efficiently without it taking up too much time.

Those are my principles, and if you like them ... well, I have others ...

So (almost!) said the great Groucho Marx. The Four Ps introduced above are the core principles that will establish and sustain musical learning from the first to the last lesson. We now need to continue our search for further principles to shape more broadly our lessons and teaching.

The five principles introduced below are in no way secondary or less important than the Four Ps. They provide the teaching environment in which the Four Ps can grow and prosper.

1 Teaching is a serious matter ...

Although teaching and learning are indeed serious matters, **all lessons should be fun and pleasurable**. This is the first of the additional principles. It doesn't mean that we need to provide a joke a minute. Lessons can still be serious and packed brimful with hard work, but delivered in a positive and enjoyable fashion. When pupils are having fun, their motivation is high and their confidence grows. Their minds and bodies will be relaxed and they will learn easily.

In fact, for effective learning, it is *imperative* that pupils maintain a positive attitude. There are a number of psychological states of mind in which pupils may find themselves during the learning process. At the top and desirable end is *knowing*. They know they can do something and thus are happy about it. If they don't yet know it but believe that they can do it – it just needs a little (or perhaps a lot!) more practice and understanding to get there – that's still fine.

But if they don't believe they can do it, and, more crucially, don't know how to achieve it, then comes *frustration* (though this is not to be confused with a kind of positive frustration which may occur at the time just before success, perhaps from necessary repetitive practice of a technical challenge or a particular passage). They have moved into the undesirable area. Frustration can lead to *anger* (and all kinds of physical tensions) and anger can lead to *depression*. Once students are in that state they probably want to throw their instruments out of the window and give up. There is no longer any pleasure to be gained.

Keeping our pupils in the *knowing* or *believing* state is therefore vitally important. So is avoiding the other three states – at all costs. Once anyone enters the frustration/anger/depression zone the purpose of learning is lost. By adopting the *High satisfaction teaching methods* (see *Improve Your Teaching!* chapter 2) pupils will remain in the *knowing* or *believing* states. We are working from their strengths, making appropriate connections, presenting calculated challenges and ensuring that they understand what they are doing. In this way they will always feel positive about their learning and so they will learn much more effectively.

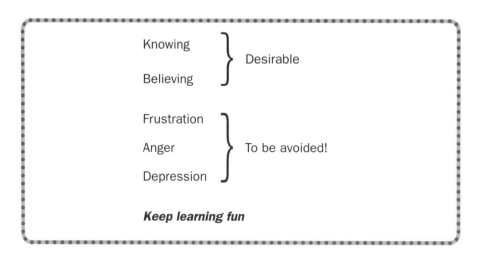

2 Be creative

The second principle is that lessons should always be infused with creative thought and activity. **Creativity is central to the development of a young musician**. Most children are tremendously creative in their thinking. Sometimes that is forgotten (or just ignored).

But first of all, *we* must strive to be creative, both when we teach technique and when we are working on the development of musicality. On the technical side, in teaching pupils how to get from A to B (or from not being able to do something to being able to do it) we will need to draw on our imaginations to produce logical sequences of related activities and to make relevant connections. Perhaps we will have to make up a sequence of extra exercises to help a struggling pupil cross the break on the clarinet, move up to third position on the violin or put the 'thumb under' on the piano. This becomes so much easier when we are thinking imaginatively and, when we are teaching something time and time again, adds an element of challenge and fun.

When it comes to musical and expressive matters, we will constantly need to draw on appropriate metaphors to help pupils bring their music to life (see also *Improve Your Teaching!* chapter 4). Knowing your pupils and their particular interests will help enormously here: how many useful football metaphors can you think up for your football-fan pupils?

Similarly, pupils must always be encouraged to be creative. They should spend part of each and every practice making things up, from their very first session onward. By creating pieces based on the particular ingredients that formed the most recent lesson or on some particular ingredients of the piece they are currently learning, pupils will find making up their own music both natural and exciting. In English lessons pupils might read a poem and then write their own based on some aspect of that poem – the title, the sentiment, the structure or the style. Make this a regular part of music teaching too. All pupils should be given the confidence to make up their own music. It's really not difficult and the earlier we introduce this kind of creativity the better.

It may be that some teachers and pupils worry about notating their own music. Indeed this may be such a concern that it inhibits the use of improvisation and composition in the early stages of teaching a beginner. The music needn't be written down at all, it could simply remain improvised or perhaps notated using some kind of simplified graphic notation (see chapter 8). If the concepts of improvisation and composition are introduced before notation, then the concern will never arise.

Perhaps there may be a further concern that spending time improvising doesn't display discernible improvement to the fee-paying parents (in contrast with the apparent improvement working at stage 1 this week and getting on to stage 2 the following week). A little explanation on the vital importance of developing the creative mind should allay all such fears.

For many teachers improvising and composing fall outside their comfort zone; like stepping into anything unknown, improvising and composing can cause stress. But in the simple act of daily conversation we are improvising all the time. Musical improvisation will come just as naturally – have a go, and remember, you can't be wrong! We'll explore these two invaluable areas of music teaching in more detail in chapters 7 and 8.

3 Practising is fun

The principle of **regular practice** between lessons must be established as early as possible. But let's move away from enticing pupils to practise because (as we tell them and their parents) 'If you practise, you'll improve and eventually you'll pass exams and give lovely performances'. 'What?! Why not?' I hear you saying. The fact is that the mention of some distant outcome is unlikely to inspire a young person to practise. Most young people are only concerned with NOW! We need to encourage pupils to practise because it is FUN. Never mind (for the moment) distant outcomes!

In chapter 2 we will see how the very first practice session, between lesson one and two, can be filled with entertaining activities based on the Four Ps. If we are teaching using the *Simultaneous Learning*[1] method, we will be encouraging practice to begin (just as our lessons do) with musicianship and aural activities leaving the tutor (or any other books) sitting quietly unopened in the music case. We teach our pupils to *think* about the lesson, about the various musical ingredients that we explored and to use these to launch into some creative activity.

[1] The two principles of Simultaneous Learning are that *everything connects* and that we teach *through the ingredients*. You will find lots of explanations and descriptions of Simultaneous Learning throughout this book, but *Improve Your Teaching!* (Faber Music) is almost entirely devoted to discussing the method.

Be sure to delve with interest into all the work that has been done during the previous week's practice. And use it to connect into the next lesson. From the very first time you talk about practice, make sure that pupils don't have the notion that it's simply all about 'repeating things to make them better'. Of course technical work will have to be done, but practice is also about exploration and imaginative thinking. It is a time for pupils to enter confidently into a magical world through their early efforts at music making. At this stage, practice is the time for our pupils to begin developing their musical understanding. Practising 'to improve' comes later.

After a while, and with consistent reinforcement, pupils will be instinctively and regularly monitoring the Four Ps themselves during their practice. And as pupils develop, we might (at an appropriate time) like to introduce and actually label the principles more formally. They make an excellent 'checklist' of good habits during practice.

4 How well am I doing?

The fourth of these additional principles is to teach our pupils the gentle art of **self-evaluation**. In fact for effective practice, it's essential. It won't normally happen overnight, but by careful and continual reminders and reinforcement we can begin to instil this tremendously useful habit. There are two elements to consider in developing an ability for self-evaluation. The first is that pupils need to understand what they are doing. This means we have to teach carefully, thoroughly and effectively. Short-cut teaching (see chapter 9) must be avoided. The second element is that they learn to do some active thinking, albeit initially at a very basic level. The way in to self-evaluation is to teach pupils to approach activities along the simple lines of:

What am I going to do?

Pupil does it, then thinks:
Did I do it well?
Could I have done it better?
Did I use the time well?

So it becomes very important that we set up the activity carefully in the lesson and explain and demonstrate what 'doing it well' is like.

In the practice session that follows pupils might, as they set off on some work on pulse, think:

I'm going to clap 12 times like a clock chiming.

Pupil claps.

I think they were all even. I can now clap evenly like a clock (and a good musician!).

Once our pupils are beginning to evaluate their work, we can begin to think about how we might develop the principle. Here is a more sophisticated model for self-evaluation:

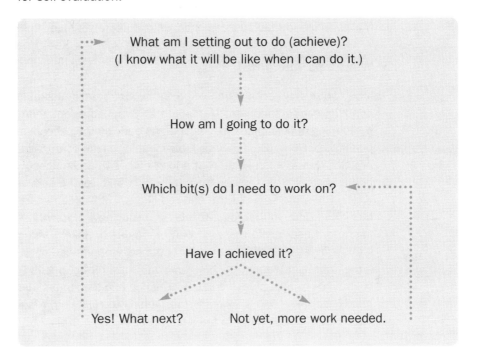

What am I setting out to do (achieve)?
(I know what it will be like when I can do it.)

How am I going to do it?

Which bit(s) do I need to work on?

Have I achieved it?

Yes! What next?   Not yet, more work needed.

Consider this model and particularly how we can encourage pupils to build up this ability.

Teaching pupils to think during their practice will reap many rewards. Besides being given the ability to sense their own achievements they will begin to think more effectively about their creative work ...

Imagine that you explored long and short notes in the lesson (among other ingredients). In the following practice session your pupil decides to:

'… make up a piece called *Stepping over stones* using C, D and E. It's going to have some long and some short notes, to be like long and short steps.'

Self-evaluating that kind of work doesn't require any assessment of whether the piece was good or bad – such assessment is entirely invalid. Indeed value-judgement thoughts of any sort would not occur to the pupil. But our pupil might think, 'That was great!' or, 'I'm going to have another go because I want more short steps', or, 'I only used the note E once and I think it might sound better with more Es'.

This kind of thinking is exactly where we want our pupils to go. It's positive and meaningful, self-enthusing and really *creative*. Indeed the more we think about the activities in which we are engaged, the more we enjoy them.

5 What a performance!

Most young children love to perform. So before adolescence and self-consciousness take root (for some anyway), present them with as many performing opportunities as possible. As early as the second lesson encourage pupils to perform. Be it their first composition made up during their first week's practice or just a long note (but a long note with an imaginative connotation – perhaps a colour, a temperature, a taste, a texture or a combination of these: 'Make your note sound warm and red like a soft woollen scarf'). Make it clear that 'This time you're going to *perform* your new piece (or long note)'. Then listen to these 'performances' with enthusiasm, delight and much enjoyment – this is not the time for a critical response. Heap praise upon the performers – they can't be wrong. In this way you'll be helping pupils to build up their confidence to take pleasure in performance and to express themselves without fear. Encourage pupils to perform regularly to relatives, friends and to other pupils. Try to organise informal concerts from time to time.

For pupils who have access to the appropriate technology, suggest they regularly record their performances (either on audio alone, or on video). Not only will this form a treasured collection and chronicle of their progress, it will also do much to motivate and assist self-evaluation.

Add all this together and you will begin to engender a real **love for performing** – the fifth, and arguably the most important of our additional principles.

So two groups of principles have now clearly emerged. The Four Ps that will form the underlying framework for all our teaching and the five 'environmental' principles that will allow us to teach positively and effectively. Now let's see how to put them into practice and how the first few, crucial lessons will develop.

A framework for teaching

The Four Ps

- Posture
- Pulse
- Phonology
- Personality

The Five 'Environmental' Principles

- All lessons should be fun and pleasurable
- Be creative
- The importance of regular practice
- Self-evaluation
- A love for performing

Points to ponder

- To what extent do you already employ the Four Ps in your teaching? How might you develop your teaching to make more use of them?

- How can you keep your pupils in the knowing or believing state?

- Find the introduction of a new technical feature in your favourite tutor book and make up some additional (creative) exercises to help reinforce the technique.

- How will you ensure that practice remains an entertaining, engaging and fun experience?

- How can we be sure that pupils are evaluating their work?

- What range of performance opportunities can you envisage for your pupils?

2 The initial stage: teaching the first lessons

There is no other lesson quite like the very first lesson. Pupils will be full of excitement and anticipation. It is the first step in what should turn out to be a wonderful, life-long journey. It is very important to make it special.

Get to know your pupil

All lessons will begin with some conversation. In the first lesson you need to discover some of your new pupil's interests. What is his or her favourite food, taste, colour, smell, sport or animal ...? This kind of information will be invaluable in coming up with appropriate analogies, images and metaphors to aid explanation and understanding. At some point during the lesson, perhaps near the end, ask 'What do you like about music?' and listen carefully to the reply: it may be very revealing.

- *'I like the sound it makes.'*

- *'I love the sound it makes.'*

- *'It makes me want to dance.'*

- *'I want to be able to play like my brother.'*

- *'It makes me feel good.'*

And of course there's always the possibility that the answer may be, *'I don't ... my mum says I've got to learn'*!

Make a regular point of asking 'What did you enjoy most in today's lesson?' Make a note of the answer. The information will help you design lessons which get the best from your pupils. It may also indicate what worked and what didn't and encourage you to devise ever more alternative and imaginative teaching strategies!

Recipe for the first lessons[2]

[2] Don't worry if the 'lessons' described in chapters 2, 3, 4 and 5 take a lot more than a single week. There may be enough to do in each one for two, three or more weeks' work.

The Four Ps, our principles of process, will infuse *every single* lesson that any pupil will ever have, literally from first to last. Put this book down now for a few moments and think specifically how you could introduce each of these principles into the first lesson. Keep the ideas and activities *really* simple. Angle your thinking towards what you'd like your pupils to take away with them to practise between the first and second lesson.

Posture There shouldn't be any problem in conveying whatever is appropriate to your instrument. Aim for a posture that is as tension-free as possible. After you've made your explanations, ask your pupil to teach *you* (or, if you are group teaching, another member of the group) how to stand, sit or hold the instrument. Be a poor student – it's more fun! Posture leads to technique and you may wish to go further (for example, introducing appropriate technical exercises) depending on the disposition of the particular pupil. But not at the expense of any of the other principles.

> *Practice* Pupils teach a parent, friend or sibling good posture. Pupils *think* about their posture and, if you introduced any simple technical exercises in the lesson, perhaps do their first repetitive practice.

Pulse Begin the teaching of pulse by exploring our own pulse. (Make the connection between our pulse and musical pulse.) Teach pupils to feel their own pulse. Then get them to think the pulse (perhaps like a throb in their head) and finally to clap it. Keep going for a while then discuss the *idea* of pulse. Now clap a steady moderate pulse and ask pupils to join in as soon as they can.

> Here are some games to get you going. *(Vary the pulse when working at these activities, even in the first lesson.)*
>
> - Teacher claps two beats, pupils echo – continue until you feel the fun begins to fade a little! Use different combinations of loud and soft. Extend to four claps.
> - Pupil claps four, then thinks four (repeat three or four times).
> - Count 1 2 3 4 – very steadily and continually, aloud first then silently mouthed and finally internally.
> - Count 1 2 3 4 steadily and continually, clapping on a particular number (beginning with 1). Do this activity counting aloud and also internally.
> - Set up a four-in-a-bar pulse. Teacher claps three out of four and pupil fills in the gap. For example:
>
>

Continue with any other pulse games you may know, using ever more sophisticated ones as pupils assimilate the concept.

When introducing the idea of clapping in a musical context make sure pupils:

- clap gently
- keep the physical movement small, neat and relaxed (watch for stiffness)
- make the movement well-defined, concentrated and rhythmic.

[3] See *Dalcroze Today* by Marie-Laure Bachmann (OUP); it's a very interesting book.

If you know any simple Dalcroze[3] rhythmic activities, these would be highly appropriate. Or just bounce a ball or play catch (in time and to music if you have technology such as a CD player available).

> *Practice* Pupils make up a piece called (for example) *The clock chimes 37* and clap 37 steady pulses (the number of chimes could change each practice session). Or play any of the pulse games above (perhaps with a relative or friend).

Phonology This is going to depend very much on your instrument. But there is no instrument that can't usually be persuaded to make some sounds after even just one lesson. The important factor is to encourage pupils to make the best sound they can – even at this extremely elementary stage. Depending on the instrument, once a sound can be made you can experiment with short and long sounds, perhaps high and low sounds and loud and soft sounds.

> *Practice* Pupils try to make *the best sound they can* at home. They can also experiment (depending on the instrument) with high/low, long/short, and loud/soft sounds. If the technology is available, they can record their sounds.

Personality Once a sound has been produced (easy on keyboard and string instruments, may take slightly longer on wind and brass instruments), try making a sleepy, calm sound (oboists might struggle here) or an angry sound; a hot or a cold sound; a sweet or a spicy sound; a dark blue or a yellow sound. Straightaway pupils are making music. What about a (musical) conversation between a grumpy elephant and a cheerful mouse? By engaging both our own and our pupil's imaginations there's no end to the possibilities.

> *Practice* Pupils make up little sound-stories, sound-pictures or musical 'cartoons' with whatever notes or sounds they have learnt to control. Even just playing around with one note will do.

The actual manner in which this lesson may unfold will depend on four main factors:

- *the age of the pupil(s)*

- *the musical experience of the pupil(s)*
  Age and musical experience will determine just how you introduce the Four Ps to your pupils. If, for instance, they play another instrument, pulse may already be understood – but take nothing for granted! Some pupils will pick up the fundamentals very fast and will want to move quickly. Even in such cases don't teach too much!

- ***the practical possibilities that your instrument offers***
  The number of different notes a pupil could reasonably be expected to play, for example – many on the piano, fewer on trumpet. Be open-minded, though: don't forget you can explore notes beyond those introduced in the first lessons in your preferred tutor. On certain instruments (particularly the piano and string instruments) pupils should be able to play many more than those typically introduced in a 'Lesson One'.

- ***the length of the lesson***
  This will of course also determine just how much you can include. Always have half an eye on the clock. Make sure there is time for all the Four Ps to be introduced and well-understood and only go further when these are firmly established.

There is one more activity which must form part of the lesson. Some teachers are fully at home with it. Others are more dubious and view it with a certain suspicion, as though it's not quite the thing to introduce into 'proper instrumental teaching', especially if they themselves are a little wary of it. It is (as you may have guessed) ... ***improvisation***.

What are the possibilities on your instrument? Let's take the piano as an example. When new pupils enter the room for their first lesson, full of huge enthusiasm and excited anticipation, and see the piano with what must be at least a thousand notes on it, they are certainly not going to be satisfied with being sent home to practise a short piece just using Middle C. They want to play ALL the notes! And so they can. They can make up anything they like. Use any notes they like. Improvise to their hearts' content.

Perhaps it may be *Battle of the monsters* or *Journey into outer-space*, *Thunderstorms* or *Raindrops*. Engage imagination and stand back! And don't forget that whatever pupils do will be highly praiseworthy. They can't be wrong. If treated and reacted to in a positive way, this kind of work can bring about enormous increases in confidence which will eventually be applied to all aspects of a pupil's music making.

Try to make a connection here with pulse, for ideally we should encourage our pupils to improvise both in time as well as freely. It is extremely important, in these very early stages of learning, that the idea of a steady pulse really is established. Perhaps you might extend the work on *The clock chimes* (from 'Pulse' above) and improvise *The clock goes wrong!*

We shall explore improvisation more fully in later chapters.

Recipe for the first practice

We want pupils to perceive practice as a fun activity (though there's little chance that they won't at this early stage!). Give them lots of engaging and imaginative things to do (see above). So for their first week's practice this is how your pupil's notebook might read:

- Be the teacher and teach (a relative or friend) how to sit properly at the piano.

- Repeat those finger exercises until they are really even.

- Make up a piece called *Midnight* where the clock strikes 12 steady chimes. Clap it and play it.

- Play the notes you've learnt today with the best sound you can.

- Play the notes calmly, angrily, heavily, lightly …

- Make up your own music.

Note down what you might expect and want *your* pupils to do in their first week's practice, depending on their instrument:

Sit there for the present …

… a teacher once told one of her pupils. But the present of course never came and the pupil was left confused and disappointed.

We need to be very careful about the words we use. If we *think* we're being understood, but in fact we're *not*, much confusion can develop! Have another look at the notebook page above. It may all seem to make sense at first glance. But maybe there's something there that's not quite comprehensible to our young pupils? 'Tunes' would be better than 'exercises' (which might suggest the gym). Will pupils understand what is meant by 'really even'? Have you explained the word 'note' (which pupils will have heard used in a number of different ways – 'make a note in your notebooks')? Being really alert to the words we use can hugely aid a pupil's development. One misunderstood word in that sequential and cumulative process that is 'learning' may result in a serious problem much further along the way.

Think also about the potential confusion over other words with both a musical and a non-musical meaning. Here are some of the words we will probably use in the early stages of learning, together with one of the meanings with which a child might automatically make a connection (there may be others):

- key (door)
- note (book)
- time (of day)
- bar (iron; adult beginners may have other thoughts ...)
- beat (in a game or race)
- tone (ringtone)
- pitch (football or baseball)

Individual, group or whole class teaching?

Whether you teach your instrument individually, in small groups or even in a whole class, always build your first lesson entirely around the Four Ps. Naturally the time you devote to each activity will vary: the larger the group, the less material overall you will probably be able to cover. And the manner in which you introduce the ingredients will vary. In a group lesson you may feel the weighting of each of the Four Ps to be different compared with an individual lesson. Depending on the instrument in question, you might wish, for example, to spend more time in Lesson One establishing posture and pulse, concentrating more on the other two principles in the next lesson. But ensure they are all introduced.

Squaring it with parents

You may find it useful to chat with parents to explain what's going on. They may have themselves been taught an instrument in a more formal, rigid and less imaginative way. 'Where did it get them?' might be an interesting line of conversation! Telling parents that our objective is to create a life-long love of music and the confidence ultimately to be musically independent is a purpose which is fairly difficult to disagree with.

Where's the tutor book?

Many parents (and pupils) will be expecting you to use a tutor book from the first lesson. Indeed the possession of the tutor book can be perceived as a strong statement of intent; an exciting (and usually shiny) accessory that tells friends of the new pursuit. But rather than plunge directly into the tutor we can explain that the first few lessons will lay extremely strong foundations that could take pupils a long way. 'We will be using a book soon', you might tell them, 'but in a little while; there are one or two important things we need to do first ...' It is to be hoped that the teachers who use really *musical* and creative methods will be those most sought out by parents and schools.

But from the very first lesson we must arm pupils with a manuscript book (a shiny one if possible) and preferably with big staves, and a notebook. Although these are traditional tools, how we use them will be of considerable importance and significance.

A moment for reflection

Let's take a little time at this point to consider some very important (and perhaps deeply revealing) questions:

- What drives *your* teaching?
- What do you wish for each pupil?
- How do you rate your own success as a teacher?
- How do you rate your own success as a performer? And what effect does this have on your teaching?

Here's another question which might help answer some of the above. What passes through your mind at the *end of your first lesson* with a new pupil (or group of pupils)?

1 It'll be six months before this pupil can take Grade One.

2 It'll be at least a year before this pupil can take Grade One.

3 This pupil will never get to Grade One ...

4 This pupil is very musical, I'm going to enjoy the next ten years.

5 This pupil is very unmusical, I'm going to hate the next ten years.

6 This pupil is a fast learner.

7 This pupil is a slow learner.

8 Oh no ...!

If we adopt the idea of teaching through the Four Ps, then our thoughts will be much more along the lines of 'Now that was fun and my pupil really seemed to get the hang of all this! We've taken the first exciting step on a journey that may lead to all sorts of wonderful places!' As to the other possible reactions, let's put the idea of Grade One or any examination far out of our minds for the moment. Are you driven by exams? Let's be honest and admit that an awful lot of teachers are. Exams are fine to drop in to from time to time. But let's not be driven by them. Let's not teach simply to climb the rather narrow and restrictive exam ladder. Instead, aim to give pupils a broad-ranging musical education rich in experience and musical encounter. A musical education where they *really* get to grips with being musical and *really understand* what they are doing.

All children are musical ...

... and providing a first lesson based on the Four Ps should allow them to find their *basic* musicality, ready for development. So we shouldn't find ourselves thinking answer five in the list above. Truly unmusical children don't exist! As to answers six and seven, neither really matters. If you are already acquainted with the basic principles of Simultaneous Learning you will be well equipped to deal with the fastest or the slowest learner. Both are challenging, and both are deeply satisfying to teach. As to answer number eight ...

Don't be too quick with the labels

Teachers are often too quick to label pupils – this one's musical, that one unmusical, this one's a slow learner, that one a quick learner and so on. Exactly what criteria and standards are being used to make such pronouncements? Labels stick, and can be very damaging. If pupils seem to display neither natural ability nor potential from the first lesson, should we exclude them? If pupils show no interest at all, then that's another matter (though again a note of caution – sometimes young children can send out complex messages: the surface may be negative, but deeper down there may be a strong desire to learn). One pupil of mine initially showed only slight interest (and hardly ever practised) but went on to study at a music conservatoire. Some pupils come to their first lessons with masses of enthusiasm, energy and potential. But if they don't, let's not write them off too quickly by making assumptions.

So what does drive your teaching?

Ideally it should be a powerful desire to give each pupil the key to unlocking a life-long love of music; it should be to help each pupil find his or her own entry into our world; it should be to find the way to give each pupil the understanding to establish and maintain an independent musical life. And that is how we should rate our success as teachers too. A pupil who has scraped through Grade Three and then gives up can't really be classed a success. Do you ever meet adults who have had that kind of experience? 'If only I'd stuck at it', they say. But perhaps they would have stuck at it if the experience had been different.

Very few of our pupils will turn into the next Menuhin or Ashkenazy, Vengarov or Kennedy, Benny Goodman or Miles Davis, Lennon or McCartney. But let's give them a chance by teaching them to be musicians. We're not just piano teachers or clarinet teachers. We teach *music* through our chosen instrument and we're teaching our pupils to be musicians through their chosen instruments. We're giving them a chance to shine. And commencing the journey with the Four Ps will give them a strong foundation.

Points to ponder

- What will you expect your pupils to do in their first week's practice?
- What qualities do you want to see in your beginners?
- What motivated you to become a teacher?
- What drives *your* teaching now?
- Has your motivation changed? If so, why?
- What do you like about teaching?
- What do you like about music?

3 The next stage: beyond the first lesson(s)

A big question that we must now consider is this: at what point should we introduce the tutor book and with it, of course, notation?

When developing our own language skills we learn to speak far sooner than we learn to read. When teaching music we tend to do both virtually at the same time. Many teachers turn to page one of their preferred tutor book almost immediately a new pupil has entered the room, eagerly awaiting the joys and adventures of the very first lesson.

But I hope that we may now feel a principle-led first lesson is a better way in, allowing us to lay down the foundations that could potentially take our pupils a long way down the instrumental-learning path. Teaching based on those principles also allows more freedom in what we actually do and greater potential for more individual and personalised instruction. Consequently we might feel able and confident to save up the tutor book for just a little longer. The great advantage is that *we* have now taken ownership of the teaching, not the tutor!

[4] Don't forget, each of these 'lessons' may take one, two or more weeks.

The main focus of 'Lesson Two'[4] is to amplify and develop the work done in the first lesson, which has subsequently been explored further in the first week's practice by the pupil at home. It is the time to monitor whether our pupils have really assimilated and understood the Four Ps. If they have, then we safely move on in the knowledge that the foundations truly are in place. If they haven't, then we must spend more time drawing on our imaginations, creating further activities and helping bring about understanding where there may still be some uncertainty.

Recipe for a second lesson

First of all we should look at how each of the Four Ps may be monitored and developed:

Posture Are there any tensions creeping in? Ask pupils to evaluate their own postures. Check (discreetly) the neck and shoulders and the way pupils are sitting at the piano or standing and holding their instruments. Correct any faults immediately, taking care over the language we might use. Rather than: 'You're not sitting properly! *This* is the correct way!', try the more friendly: 'How about sitting like this? You'll probably find it a lot easier and more comfortable.'

If pupils come to the second clarinet or flute lesson with the wrong hand position or playing the piano with the sides of their fingers or holding the violin with their right hand and bow in the left, we need to take care over how we react. The manner in which we correct faults should be kindly and imaginative. Our pupil may have worked hard and be full of expectation for praise and congratulations. A negative reaction may be destructive and upsetting, so perhaps we might say something like: 'Well that's certainly an interesting way to do it! But why not try it like this instead …'.

You may have introduced some technical work in the first lesson. If so, work through it to see that it has been fully absorbed and understood and then connect it carefully with some new work, always explaining clearly (making as few assumptions as possible) and double-checking to see whether pupils have fully grasped it. You can do this, for example, by reversing positions: pupil teaches teacher. In this way we can monitor if our pupils really understand and also catch a glimpse into their own processing of the information by the language they use. Technique must be taught *very carefully*: anything misconstrued at this stage may take weeks (or months or even years) to unravel.

Remember that one of the best ways to teach technique is through demonstration. Young pupils need to see how it's done as well as being told. Their natural instinct is to copy. However, I have (albeit very rarely) seen teachers spend far too much time demonstrating – it can become a vehicle for showing off or inflating egos. It happens when teachers are bored and will almost always result in pupils becoming disinterested.

Also bear in mind that we can teach pupils to practise physical movements mentally as well as physically. Recent scientific research has shown that just thinking about moving fingers (a five-finger exercise for example) can have a marked effect on developing technique.

Pulse We want to hear that the concept of a steady pulse has been absorbed – talk to pupils about the way they practised *The clock chimes* and ask for a performance. 'Was it really steady?' Perhaps perform it yourself with some hurrying or unevenness. Could they hear the unevenness? Which part of the performance was unsteady? Can pupils describe the *idea* of a steady pulse?

Now with the instrument, develop the clock idea further: make up a piece using two notes to represent the tick-tock sound of a clock. Experiment with trying to convey different types of clock: Grandfather, Grandmother, mantelpiece and wristwatch. Perhaps you might introduce a metronome at this point! There are interesting connections to be made. A pulse of ♩ = 60 would probably be most appropriate for this activity.

We now need to introduce the idea of metre. Here are some ideas.

- Ask pupils to clap in groups of four beats with a strong emphasis on the first. Teach pupils how to beat four-in-a-bar.
- Set up a four-in-a-bar pulse then ask pupils to *count in their head* ('we're going to count in patterns like this: **1** 2 3 4 **2** 2 3 4 **3** 2 3 4 …'). Pupils then clap aloud (or play a note) on, for example, the second beat of the fifth bar. This activity is particularly fun when played in groups (with eyes closed!).
- Evolve some rhythms and rhythm games based on pupils' names and interests. For instance:

Having clapped the rhythm a number of times, you could:
- Alternately clap the rhythm and then hear it in your head.
- Tap (on a table or piano lid) 'James Bond' with the right hand followed by 'plays the piano' with the left. Then reverse.
- Clap 'James Bond' and ask the pupil to respond with 'plays the piano'.
- Re-organize the rhythm and clap 'Plays the piano James Bond'.

- Once that has been grasped all sorts of fun is possible: 'James plays the Bond piano'; 'James plays the piano Bond'. Or perhaps clap some and *think* some: 'James ___ plays the __ __' , ending up with '_____ _____ _____ __ __-no'!

- Setting up a four-in-a-bar pulse, make up a conversation between two people, one angry and the other calm. It might begin something like this:

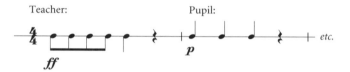

- Now with the instrument make up some pieces using the rhythms. Mix them with other ingredients as technique will allow – loud and soft, with accents or using different notes.

- Improvise more 'conversations' with instruments.

Just a brief word on vocabulary: are we going to use the word *rhythm*? Some pupils will understand this. For others (and especially younger beginners) the word *pattern* is a useful alternative in the early stages.

Phonology The work we will be doing on sound will now be very much linked with both technique and the fourth P (personality). Whatever technical work we introduce, ensure that pupils are *listening* to the sound they are making and that they are always trying to make the best sound they can. Demonstrate often – pupils need a sound to aspire to – using short examples. You might like to discuss what a 'good sound' is considered to be. Are they listening to beginnings and endings of notes? If they are producing sustained sounds (wind, strings and brass) pupils should also listen carefully for evenness.

Personality Listen to anything (sounds, pieces, improvisations) that has been prepared during the week's practice and use it to suggest further activities. Using either free rhythmic ideas or rhythms made up from word-phrases, ask pupils to improvise little pieces with interesting titles: *Taking a hippopotamus for a walk*, for example. Or make up a simple story and improvise music to go with it. Decide which kind of ingredients are to be used (depending on what pupils are able to do at this stage) perhaps choose from loud/soft, long/short, accented/non-accented notes, high/low, single notes, repeated notes, rhythms based on words. Don't forget to play to pupils (cheerful and gloomy pieces, fast and slow pieces) so that they have frequent opportunities to enjoy and respond to the power of music.

There's plenty of material here for the second lesson. If you and your pupils really get involved in this kind of teaching and learning you'll find it is easy to fill the time. You may wish to introduce the tutor book in this lesson. My own preference is to delay it just a little bit longer.

In summary, during the course of this lesson we are:
- further establishing the Four Ps
- working hard
- being musical
- being creative
- using the work prepared in practice and suggesting new ideas for the next practice
- enjoying some performances
- giving pupils the opportunity to listen to music
- getting pupils to evaluate their work

and, above all, *having fun*.

Simultaneous Learning and practice

The two fundamental principles of Simultaneous Learning are that *everything connects* and that we should always be teaching *through the ingredients*. The result of this kind of teaching is that pupils really understand what they are doing and are then able to apply their understanding. If we are using the methods and strategies described above, we are already teaching *simultaneously*. At this stage, because we are dealing with limited ingredients, we need only make simple connections. If pupils apply the angry/calm rhythmic conversation (above) to notes on their instruments, thinking about the quality of the sounds and doing this with good posture, they are already connecting all Four Ps.

Practice in week two will be concerned with working on any more technical areas you may have introduced, playing more pulse and rhythm games, refining sounds and then mixing everything together by improvising little sound pictures, stories or characters: whatever or wherever pupils' imaginations take them.

Always ask pupils what they enjoyed in their practice. Though we don't wish to encourage any negative thinking it may be helpful to ask them if there was anything they didn't enjoy or found difficult. Both questions may be answered in their first response. These answers may be very useful in guiding you to shape the next lesson or in your approach to discussing their next practice.

And so the journey continues ...

Points to ponder

- How will you develop the Four Ps further in the second lesson?
- What kind of technical work might you introduce in the second lesson?
- What are your thoughts on when to introduce the tutor book?

4 Introducing the tutor book

❝ Telling them all about it is not teaching …
making them observe and discover is teaching. ❞
Preface to the ninth edition of Mrs Curwen's *Pianoforte Method*, 1900

All good teaching is built on effective interaction between teacher and pupil. The style of teaching described in the first three chapters moves away from a purely teacher-led approach where teacher instructs and pupils obey. And because we don't open the tutor book straight away, we also move away from a tutor-book-led approach. And as we are teaching 'out of our heads', rather than 'out of the book', we also receive greater respect from our pupils.

We may like to take pupils on further using the methods introduced above. In so doing we allow the Four Ps, musicianship, technical and creative skills to develop in a very valuable way. Some pupils may benefit hugely from a continuation of this type of teaching – perhaps even for the whole first term. But we may feel that reading skills should also become part of the training.

We are all familiar with the problems generated by teaching methods that rely heavily on playing by ear. Whilst these methods may produce young players of (sometimes) dizzyingly spectacular technical proficiency, the difficulties encountered when the same pupils hit the ground with a bump as they begin to grapple with notation are well known. There are clearly considerable benefits in learning to play and read more or less at the same time. Thus we open the tutor book. But we open it with a creative mind!

And with the tutor now open, make good use of it, but have the courage to deviate, add or substitute your own exercises or pieces, move sideways (or indeed in any direction!) as you feel appropriate. Don't feel that you have to begin right at the beginning – you may well wish to skip the introductory pages (if there are any). The work we have done in the first lessons possibly renders them redundant anyway. Remember that the tutor is an accessory to our teaching – not the sole driving force.

The main reason for opening the tutor is to introduce pupils to notation and repertoire. Almost certainly they will be able to read words. So get them to do just that before tackling the music for the first time. There are bound to be some preliminary words near the beginning of the book. Then discuss what the pupils just did. They read the words silently, in their heads. They 'heard' the words internally and they understood them. So they are going to do the same with the music.

Read all about it!

Here's how to teach that first piece of musical notation (whatever the instrument). The activities outlined here are not new, but it is the order in which they are presented that is crucial. Much will be gained by following the order strictly and making sure that each step is really absorbed and totally understood before moving on:

- Set up the pulse. I've often seen teaching where no pulse is ever 'set-up' – do make a habit of always setting a pulse before beginning any playing.
- Pupil claps or taps the pulse.
- Talk about the rhythm. Introduce the note values and their names, how they relate to the pulse and how to count.
- Pupil hears the rhythm *internally*, just like hearing those words a few minutes earlier.
- Pupil taps or claps the rhythm, counting aloud. An additional step would be for pupil to tap the pulse with a foot and the rhythm with the hands, or the pulse with one hand and the rhythm with the other.
- Pupil sings the rhythm (to *la*, *ta*, etc), tapping the pulse as he or she does so. Young pupils will have no qualms about this; older ones may, but persevere!
- Introduce the pitch, in other words the name of the note or notes, and play it/them to your pupil.
- Pupil reads the piece, hearing it internally, clapping the pulse.
- Pupil sings the piece, clapping the pulse.
- Now finally remind pupil how to finger/play the notes.
- Pupil has a final 'read' of the piece. Ask whether it is absolutely understood.
- Pupil plays the piece, knowing *exactly what to do* and *exactly what it's going to sound like*.

The first piece of musical notation has now been read confidently, accurately and with complete understanding, the result of really thorough teaching.

Remember to comment on posture and expect the best sound possible when playing. It will take a little time to go through these activities (and you may insert some more of your own along the way). There is no hurry and this is some of the most important teaching that your pupils will receive. It is time very well spent. You will have set up a process that should guarantee confidence in notation and (if you always set about reading new music in this way) confidence and accuracy in sight-reading too. With really careful and thorough teaching, pupils should always be able to sight-read at the same level as the pieces they are learning.

Now be creative

Having taught your pupil to read and play his or her first piece from notation don't go straight to the second but use it to lead you off in other directions, making all sorts of different connections in the Simultaneous Learning way. Depending on how much time you have available, choose from these:

- *dynamic levels*
  Add dynamic levels (as appropriate to your instrument and pupil's capabilities): play the piece as loudly as possible, as though the volume

on the TV was turned right up; then as though it's a long way away and you can only just hear it, or a combination of the two.

- **tempo**
  Try it at different speeds. Decide on and establish the pulse first. Perhaps use a metronome here.

- **musical personality**
  Play it angrily or lovingly. Encourage pupils to choose their own expression. Perhaps give the piece alternative titles.

- **imagination**
  Play it with a lemon (tart), or chocolate (sweet) sound.

- **memory**
  Play it by heart.

- **composition**
  Ask pupils to make up their own piece, with their own title, using the same ingredients (notes and rhythms). It may turn out to be very similar indeed, but it is still their own piece! Pupils should be encouraged to compose from the very first lesson (more about this in chapter 8).

- **aural**
  - Play the piece to pupils (perhaps extending it), asking pupils to clap the pulse.
  - Play the piece (or part of the piece) to pupils, but change a note. They sing it back to you and then describe how you altered it.
  - Play the piece to your pupils with more dramatic changes (change of octave, tempo, pianists might add a second part) and ask them to describe what you did.
  - The pupil plays the piece to you with a change and you have to describe it.

Whatever you don't have time for in the lesson, you might suggest the pupil tries during practice.

Through the Simultaneous Learning method, and making these natural connections, with one thing leading to another, we are teaching comprehensively, holistically and thoroughly. We've already included aural work (in a number of guises), hearing internally, rhythm work, improvisation and composition, notation and reading. And there's still one more connection we can make …

… with the write stuff

In teaching and learning language we engage cheerfully in the four connected areas of speaking and listening, reading and writing. In music most teachers and pupils are happily engaged in playing (speaking), reading and listening, but few show more than a marginal interest in writing. Some think the writing element resides in that rather dry and dusty place known as 'theory' (also often taught in a dry and dusty place). In fact we should get our pupils writing from as early as possible. Pupils will vary considerably in their ability to write, so try to discover, as discreetly as possible, what might be realistically achieved. You may get a pupil, at the very least, to draw a semibreve or minim (or whatever note length is introduced in the first lesson) or, at the other end of the spectrum, they may be able to write out their own composition based on the one they are learning from the tutor.

Minim =
half note

Semibreve =
whole note

Whatever your pupils have written down ask them to play it from their own notation. In this way you will be helping them to make and form strong connections:

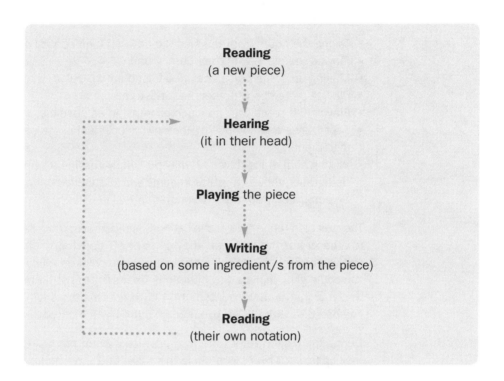

Reading
(a new piece)

Hearing
(it in their head)

Playing the piece

Writing
(based on some ingredient/s from the piece)

Reading
(their own notation)

Encourage the habit of writing something down each lesson and make sure it is directly connected to what pupils are learning. It will reap rich rewards.

Some pupils may feel what they can or cannot write imposes limits on their composing. Their view of composition somehow begins to be dictated by their ability to notate their music. Given even just a little encouragement many pupils may be creating all kinds of sonic masterpieces. They must not be discouraged! If they are keen to notate their more complex creations the solution probably lies in using some form of graphic notation (see chapter 7).

... and so to practice

This lesson (it may be lesson three or you may have saved it up for later) has been based around teaching our pupils their first piece using notation. But we've done it with the Four Ps strongly evident and in the Simultaneous Learning way. We've made connections to aural, theory, memory, improvisation and various other musical ingredients. And we may have introduced more technical work too.

Practice should take the piece (or pieces) from the tutor book as the point of departure. Pupils should be guided towards:

- Taking the notes from the piece to develop their control of sound.
- Playing the piece with their best sound.
- Making up some pulse activities based on the pulse of the piece.
- Playing the piece with their best posture.
- Playing the piece with as much expression as possible.
- Improvising and composing their own pieces using the same ingredients.
- Writing something down – it may be simply copying a symbol or it may be notating their own piece in some way. Further activities can then be generated from their own notation.

They will also refine their technical work and perhaps, if pupils have access to a library or the internet, they can set off on what might become an ongoing project about their instrument. Some children will love doing this. You could give pupils a few questions to answer to get them going: When was your instrument invented? How different was the original instrument compared to yours? Can you find a picture of an early one?

During the lesson refer (often) to practice: 'When practising at home try making up your own piece using the same title ... remember to play with your best sound ... play this counting game with a friend/relative ...'. And for how long should pupils practise? The best answer would be 'as long as they want to!' But make the point that practice should ideally take place every day and for at least ten to fifteen minutes. At this stage enthusiasm is running high and we need to make the most of it.

Points to ponder

- Think about how you're going to introduce the tutor book.
- How important do you consider music-reading skills?
- How important do you consider music-writing skills?

5 Taking stock and moving forward

At the start of this 'stage' it is important to examine carefully the success of the previous lessons. Begin with a bit of a quiz/check-up/exam (use the word to which your pupils would best respond). Or you may not even tell your pupils what you're up to!

As with all Simultaneous Learning lessons we start with aural and musicianship activities.

First of all take stock of how the Four Ps are developing:

Posture

- Have a close look at posture. Praise it if it is good or discuss and correct anything that might be a cause for concern. It is so important to spot even the smallest problems at this stage and put them right. Once poor posture is acquired it becomes more problematic to correct.

Pulse

- Ask pupils to count in bars of two in their heads (**1**-2 **2**-2 **3**-2 **4**-2) and then clap (for example) on the second beat of the seventh bar.
- Ask pupils to improvise a *March* in strict time.

Phonology

- Ask pupils to play some notes with their best sound (at different dynamic levels if possible).
- Play a piece to pupils and ask them to listen carefully to your sound and then to find some words to describe it.

Personality

- Ask pupils to play a piece they've been practising, making it as characterful or as expressive as they can. Talk about what it is they are trying to convey.
- Ask pupils to improvise a short piece that describes a relative, friend or pet. Discuss the improvisation.

Next, we need to be sure that the introductory work on notation has been fully absorbed. Before the lesson, using the very same ingredients as in the first pieces or exercises, compose a similar piece for your pupils. Write it out clearly on manuscript paper (or set it using computer notation software). Play some improvisatory call-and-response games first and then ask your pupils to study the notated piece carefully. Once they feel they have understood it ask:

- how they will count it?
- the note names
- how they will finger/produce the sounds?

Then ask them to:

- clap the piece (using both accented and unaccented claps)
- hear it internally
- sing it out loud
- play it.

Don't allow pupils to play it until they are confident it is fully understood and you are sure it will be correct. This is, in effect, their first piece of 'sight-reading'. If you always take time and prepare notation reading thoroughly, sight-reading should never (ever!) be a problem.

Using the same ingredients as in the previous piece, play pupils another very simple and short piece and then ask them to:

- repeat it from memory
- write all or some of it in the manuscript books
- make up their own piece using the same ingredients.

If all the above goes well then you can feel really confident in moving on. All this adds up to very thorough teaching – you are laying down the sturdiest of foundations which will ensure real progress.

Try to avoid writing the note names, the counting or the fingering on the music (and check that the pupil or a helpful parent doesn't either!). Reading music without these short cuts will force pupils to understand notation properly – it may take a little longer, but it's time well spent.[5]

[5] Occasional little reminders are of course fine. As are witty comments/cartoons or anything that might bring a smile to a pupil's face.

Moving on

With appropriate guidance, repetition and reinforcement of all that has been learnt so far, we are probably now ready to take on the Simultaneous Learning process more broadly. As each new piece (or even exercise) is taught, identify the ingredients – which may be technical, musical (character), specific markings, key, rhythm, or theoretical features – and work at them through aural and musicianship activities, making and explaining connections as we go along. Here's an example of how the first lesson on *Up and down* (an exercise from an imaginary clarinet tutor) might evolve:

Up and down

Paul Harris

March-like

(The book is closed.)

- Pupils play C (the key-note of the piece) as a long note. They listen carefully to the sound, aiming to play it with their best tone quality and in tune.
  The note is flat so we do some work on intonation/listening and then work at the appropriate technique to sharpen the note.

  Repeat the long note.
  It's now in tune. So move on to some work on pulse ...

- Establish a four-in-a-bar pulse. Pupils clap the pulse (with a slight accent on the first beat and the others unaccented). With pupils continuing to clap the pulse teacher plays repeated (tongued) Cs. Now exchange roles: pupils play a series of tongued Cs while teacher claps the pulse.
  The notes are too heavy – remedial work needed on lighter tonguing.

  Repeat tonguing exercise.
  When satisfied, move on to work establishing a sense of C major.

- Do some call and response – short one-bar and then two-bar phrases using the notes C D E and rests whilst maintaining the pulse. Make the phrases march-like.
  Pupils do well so ...

- Discuss the character of the playing in the previous activity. Play the micro-scale[6] of C major (CDEDC) tongued, still in the same pulse and with a march-like feel.
  Pupils play well so ...

[6] Microscales can be either the first three or five notes of a scale. They offer virtually no technical problems and provide a clear sense of key.

  Repeat the scale first *f* and then *p*, still tongued and in the same pulse and character.
  Pupils play well so ...

- Do some more call-and-response work where pupils improvise the answer. Keep to the same ingredients. Begin with the actual two-bar phrase that opens *Up and down*. Change roles with pupils now 'leading'.
  Pupils play well and are confident in leading so ...

- Open the book and discuss the piece (for example the significance of the title). What can pupils recognise from the above activities?
  And so on ...

If this kind of teaching is new to you, choose a very easy piece or exercise from the tutor book you use and imagine how the lesson might unfold.

The beauty of Simultaneous Learning is that we are always setting the agenda with tasks (on the whole) our pupils *can* do. Occasionally we will have to correct and then reinforce, but it will always be within a positive process. If a pupil responded to one of the above tasks in a different way, the lesson may take an alternative route. But we would still eventually have reached the same destination. Another exciting advantage of Simultaneous Learning is that a lesson will generate its own momentum – once we get in the groove and are using our imaginations, teaching becomes both exciting and very satisfying. We have moved away from that wearisome and arduous kind of lesson where teachers spend most of their time simply reacting to pupils' mistakes. Indeed, that kind of activity can hardly be termed teaching.

So when we come to the point in the lesson where we open the book and pupils see *Up and down*, they will immediately be able to read it with understanding. They will instantly have some insight into the music. We may begin at the beginning or we may work at some feature that catches our pupil's eye. Try in fact to avoid always working from 'bar one', unless there's a particular reason for doing so. It is often much more interesting to begin elsewhere. This kind of teaching also reduces the time between first contact with a new piece and being able to play it. You'll find you can teach many more pieces.

Working in this fashion will instil confidence and comprehension.

For their practices now, pupils must be encouraged to *think* about the work of the lesson and then develop that work further. Teach pupils to spend a few minutes (at least) *with the book closed* exploring the ingredients (through making up their own little exercises and improvisations) before beginning work with the notation. Open pupils' minds to being creative.

Now all we need to do is continue to teach in this fashion. Sometimes we might concentrate on left-brain areas: technique and notation for example; sometimes more on right-brain matters[7]: aural, improvisation, memory and interpretation (always of course making connections between the two as we go along). In this way we are giving our pupils a holistic, enjoyable and comprehensible musical education.

[7] The whole fascinating subject of right- and left-brain teaching is dealt with in detail in *Improve Your Teaching!* (chapter 3). To develop the complete musician we must nurture the whole brain.

Creating a passport for a musical life

Around this time pupils should be encouraged to begin constructing their own personal musical history: a type of ID that tracks and records their individual musical experiences. It will come to represent their musical personality. It could be assembled in a diary or logbook or, preferably, electronically in a computer document and will always then be there, like a passport, if the pupil moves to another teacher, another school, even another country. It will remind pupils of all their musical encounters. Begin it by including:

- Pieces learnt.
- A list of all performances given (including those to granny after Sunday lunches).
- Selected improvisations (if recorded – audio or video – all the better).
- Progress with the Four Ps.
- Favourite pieces.

- Pieces heard (on recordings; played by friends).
- Projects undertaken (on the history or workings of the instrument or on composers, for example).
- Compositions: particularly exciting if pupils have access to, and a working ability of, computerised music notational software. They can include their own compositions for others to hear and play. Pupils can still include composition without such technology through more conventional or graphic notation.
- Pictures collected (of themselves playing perhaps, famous players, the instrument, etc.).

This will become an invaluable document.

Adding material to the tutor

As we now work through the tutor, we'll be free to add material (mostly our own), reinforcing where necessary and providing further similar examples to monitor whether pupils really have absorbed the concepts. It doesn't take long to compose such pieces, and it makes use of our creative ability. As a result, our teaching becomes still more interesting, there is more variety and it ensures that we are driving the teaching forward.

From time to time we might even make our own arrangements of a parent's favourite tune or song for birthdays or other occasions, arranging them specifically for a particular pupil's abilities. This makes a big impression on a parent who perhaps feels out of place in the serious world of instrumental teaching. It encourages parents to enjoy the results of their investment of both time and money.

Off the beaten track

Occasionally, if a particular piece takes a pupil's (or your) fancy, take time to develop it – make broader connections and be *simultaneous*! A project of this kind may last two lessons or half a term! This sort of deviation may also be useful if a pupil (for some reason) may be losing interest or is struggling with technical progress and needs more reinforcement. Teachers sometimes respond to this with 'nice idea … but I don't really have the time'. Good teaching should never be in a hurry.

For instance, you may be working on a piece called *Spanish dance*. You might:

- Work on a variety of 'Spanish-like' rhythms, both clapping and playing.
- Improvise using these rhythms.
- Write them down.
- Investigate Spanish dance on the Internet or in books from the library.
- Encourage pupils to compose their own Spanish dance. Perhaps find some castanets to accompany these pieces.
- Record other Spanish dances to listen to and discuss.
- Write a poem, draw a picture, make Spanish food.
- Learn more dance pieces.
- Arrange a little informal concert with a Spanish flavour.

The end of the first term

Pupils will vary enormously in their achievements by the end of their first term. Some will have raced through their first tutor, with everything they've learnt being fully understood. Others may still be at an elementary stage in many (or even all) areas. But if you're teaching through the Four Ps and using Simultaneous Learning, then *all* pupils will have had many musical experiences – some possibly even life-enhancing. And they will certainly all have the correct foundations on which to build their musical futures.

There are many reasons why people like learning to play an instrument, but to perform and *give pleasure* to others must be an important one. So at the end of term try to arrange an informal concert, including as many of your pupils as possible. However, it is very important that we consider what is in our pupils' minds when we talk about performing. Sometimes the pleasurable aspect gets lost even when playing to family and friends. Playing to others can become rather inward-looking from very early on if there's any anxiety, and even if there isn't. Pupils often tend to be congratulated on their performance rather than the pleasure it gives. So make sure that comments such as 'I did so much *enjoy* your playing' are as plentiful as 'You played very well'.

For the concert, short pieces are recommended (especially if you have quite a number of pupils taking part) and pupils should play pieces that they like and are well within their grasp – therefore perhaps not those most recently learnt. Introduce each piece. Some pupils may like to do this themselves, but don't insist on it if they find the idea too intimidating. Make the introductions fun. I have attended a number of these events where well-intentioned but brief and mumbled introductions destroyed any excitement or sense of occasion. Parents and friends can bring refreshments to round off what will hopefully have been a very exciting first term of music-making.

Points to ponder

- Compare your teaching at present to the Simultaneous Learning approach.

- Do you feel adopting the Simultaneous Learning style of teaching would be quite a leap to make? If so, consider how you would gradually introduce it (and the Four Ps) into your teaching.

- Do you feel comfortable with the idea of creating your own extra materials? If not, why not?

- On average, what would you normally expect of pupils at the end of their first term of lessons?

- What are the factors that determine a pupil's progress?

6 Inheriting a pupil

Often we don't have the good fortune to teach pupils from the very first lesson. When inheriting a student we do sometimes find that good foundations have been established, yet only too frequently we meet with all kinds of troubles, many that may take months (or even longer) to put right.

These troubles may come in a variety of guises:

- poor posture and technique
- poor sound quality and a general lack of tone control
- uncertain rhythmic understanding
- lack of musicianship
- poor or inappropriate motivation
- weak reading skills
- a general inability to be creative and expressive when playing.

You may be able to add additional problems to the list! Often pupils will display an alarming cocktail of the above. If they've been squeezed through an exam, then the problems can be compounded still further through having taken all manner of short cuts.

In a sense these pupils are still beginners, and this is why it is appropriate to consider such pupils in this book.

I remember a pupil arriving on the doorstep having just passed Grade One – a few marks over the pass mark – and clutching the Grade Two music purchased on the instruction of the former teacher. The pupil had spent the best part of the previous three terms learning (just) the exam pieces and reluctantly engaging with scales, sight-reading and aural – the 'medicinal stuff' as his teacher called it. ('It's not very nice but it's good for you.') It is not an uncommon scenario and I'm sure you've met such a pupil (or very similar ones) many times. It is a difficult situation to deal with.

First we need to make an assessment – though the outcome is all too predictable. We might begin with that very useful and revealing question, 'What do you like about music?' Perhaps we might follow this up with 'What do you most like in lessons?' and 'What do you most enjoy doing in your practice?' The answers could be very revealing. How does the pupil measure up to the Four Ps? A performance of a favourite piece will probably tell us all we need to know. Are reading skills on a par with playing skills? In many cases there will be a lot of remedial work to be done.

Our best course may be to make a deal with the pupil. Don't criticize the former teacher (directly anyway), but be candid and positive: 'There are a number of good things about your playing, but if you really want to do well in that next exam, we've got to sort out one or two things, maybe go back and re-think a few areas from scratch. At the end of that process you'll be so much more musically confident and technically secure. Is that okay with you?' Maybe you'll need to have the same conversation with the parent. It is unlikely that you'll receive a negative response. And once you have a 'Yes, that's okay with me', then you can get to work!

Back to the Four Ps

All you really have to do is go back to the Four Ps and work through each one carefully. In some cases you may really have to go back to the beginning. For many pupils, embarking on a Simultaneous Learning approach underpinned by the Four Ps may be very refreshing: it may seem like a new start which creates a renewed enthusiasm. This is exactly what you want.

It is important, however, to maintain a sense of security in this situation and to maintain a connection with what has gone before. So work on familiar pieces as well as introducing new repertoire. This may be the first time the pupil has engaged in musical activities without the book in front of them and it may initially feel a little unsettling. You may meet with considerable reluctance in some pupils. Persevere gently!

A cello pupil may play a piece with poor intonation, an unsteady pulse and inexpressively. Close the music book and perhaps begin by talking about the idea of playing in tune. This may take you in any number of different directions depending on what the pupil understands by the concept – it may never have been properly broached before.Then work on the scale (which may be unknown or at least never related to the piece). The pupil plays it with a strong sense of pulse; then in different moods (or colours or whatever you feel the particular pupil would respond to). Discuss the mood or character of the piece itself and then apply it to the scale. Open the music again and discuss what ingredients the composer uses to portray the character. You may wish to make more connections with other areas (concentrating first on the Four Ps) before playing the piece again. Discuss how this performance differed from the original performance. Did the pupil feel different about the performance? Was it more enjoyable to play?

It will probably take a few weeks to win the full confidence of inherited pupils, and probably a lot longer to change their attitude to the more 'medicinal' aspects of their musical education. Tread carefully at first, don't try to do too much too quickly and resist any temptation to put down the previous teacher's methods. Whatever you do, don't resort to any quick-fix or short-cut remedies. This will only make matters worse. Remedial teaching takes time and needs to be very thorough. Give your new pupil lots of easier pieces to learn while you re-teach concepts that are confused or misunderstood. Reinforce as much as necessary, never getting frustrated if progress is slow. Don't ask if the pupil has finally understood anything you've been working on – give them an activity to demonstrate their understanding. But in a relatively short time you ought to have a much more musically aware pupil with a real sense of where he or she is going, and how to get there.

Points to ponder

- Think about some pupils you've inherited and how you've reacted to their abilities (or lack of them!).
- What do you do when a pupil comes to you and says 'I only want to play for fun'?

7 Improvising – it's easy!

Get your instrument out or sit at the piano ... Now play a note. Any note.

You've just improvised.

Using the same note, infuse the sound with:
- love
- hate
- anger
- fear
- tenderness

Note that I didn't ask you to *convey* love, hate, anger or any of the other feelings in the sound. Just to infuse the sound with those (right-brain) feelings. In other words, just let those feelings flow into the sound. It also allows you to steer clear of a 'now-how-do-I-do-that?' (left-brain) kind of thinking. You are improvising creatively, being *musical*, albeit in a very simple and direct kind of way. There may not have been much difference between the various sounds. That's not important. It is the fact that these sounds were created through the imagination, through the right-brain, through your feelings.

Now, either use the same note, choose a different note or add a note, and create:
- a peppermint sound
- a hot sound
- an icy sound
- a smelly sound
- a strong black coffee sound

Again the difference in actual tone colour is less important than the fact that the imagination was brought strongly into play. But, this time, there may well have been some interesting differences ...

Using the same notes or adding more, create:
- a comma
- a full stop
- an exclamation mark
- a question mark
- a dance
- a simple melody
- a march

Did you find any of that difficult? Improvising is easy!

Think about the answers that your pupils gave to those questions (see page 16) about favourite taste, colour and smell. Even in that first lesson ask them to make a chocolate or a lemon sound, a dark blue or yellow sound or perhaps a perfumed sound. Anything will work, particularly if the ideas are based on your pupils' interests. Young children will embrace this kind of activity enthusiastically. Their open-minded imaginations will switch on and produce all sorts of interesting results. Even in just using one note they might try a dance or march. Most older children will find the ideas intriguing and will be happy to make an attempt too. There may be a number of cynics among them, but even they can be cajoled into having a go. Work from their particular interests.

This kind of truly creative work, further developed over months and years, will ultimately have a marked influence on musical thinking at all levels. It will allow pupils to play their Mozart or Brahms, Gershwin or McCartney with a musical freshness and spontaneity. An appropriate word, image or analogy may make a huge difference. A performance of any repertoire becomes more of a *creation* rather than a *re-creation*.

Musical conversations

Play 'musical conversations' often with pupils. Encourage them to respond in all sorts of different ways. Depending on the age of your pupils, discuss what can happen in a spoken conversation: people can repeat themselves, repeat what the other person just said, agree, disagree, interrupt, develop or change the subject. You can have a musical conversation along the same lines. The conversation might be friendly or angry; you might be having it when you've just woken up or when you're very tired; you could be having it at a party or in a church … Decide on the ingredients beforehand: which notes to use, the dynamic levels, short and long notes, slow or fast pulse and so on. Use the ingredients pupils are currently learning in particular pieces to make more connections. It's a lot of fun and your pupils will have a very creative experience.

Simultaneous Learning, improvisation and new pieces

By now, we should always be introducing new pieces through their ingredients. This is one of the two central principles of Simultaneous Learning. Among those ingredients are key, rhythmic patterns, dynamic markings, other markings, technical or theoretical points and character. Make a mental list and then use improvisation to experience and explore new musical concepts in the piece as well as reinforcing those already learned or understood. Always ask pupils to make their own list of ingredients from which to work. This approach will form the first part of both their practice sessions and lessons.[8] Encourage pupils to improvise their own exercises to practise technical work and always use improvisation when introducing something theoretical – an interval, a new Italian term, a rest …

[8] *Improve Your Practice!* (Faber Music) is a lively and imaginative approach to creative practice, based on Simultaneous Learning.

Here's how a new piece might be introduced using Simultaneous Learning, with particular emphasis on improvisation, and making lots of connections en route:

The rusty old wheelbarrow carries some potatoes

Paul Harris

With the actual copy out of sight, we set off on our Simultaneous Learning journey making connections:

- *with pulse (1):* establish a three-in-a-bar pulse and play call-and-response clapping games based on the rhythms of the piece.

- *with pulse (2):* using the same pulse play more call-and-response where the response (by the pupils) is now different (improvised).

- *with pulse (3):* play the piece to your pupils. They join in, first clapping the pulse and then conducting (beating) time as you play.

- *with melodic shape:* play the piece (or part of the piece) again and, using graphic, pictorial shapes, pupils 'draw' the melodic shape (in broad outline) in their notebooks. Either just the right hand or both parts!

- *with rhythm:* clap the actual rhythm of the piece in one, two or even four-bar phrases for pupils to copy.

- *with key:* pupils improvise a short piece in C major based on the rhythms used in the preceding activities. Just use the first three notes of the scale (as in the piece). One hand at a time, then hands together.

- *with the scale:* play the scale of C major (the microscale will do: the first three – or preferably – five notes) with an even rhythm and in contrary motion. Play the scale f, p, and getting louder (the dynamics used in the piece).

- *with staccato:* add staccato to the above then improvise a little piece using the first three notes above and below middle C major (both hands as in this piece) and some of the rhythms. Add a crescendo.

- *with theory:* talk about the interval of a second and explore seconds above and below middle C, melodically and harmonically. Improvise a little piece using seconds and give it a title. Write an interval of a second in manuscript books.

- *with more written theory:* write down a rhythm, the first three notes of C major, the f or p symbol – anything from the above.

- *with dynamics:* improvise two short phrases based on any of the above ingredients, the first one f and the second p.

- *with character:* improvise a little piece that 'bumps along'.

Some teachers have suggested that this sort of teaching wastes time. Nothing could be further from the truth. We are teaching in a non-threatening way using our imaginations. Pupils are learning and having fun. And by coming at each concept from so many different angles we are ensuring that the learning is thorough. Pupils will (almost always) achieve and understand.

Once you're teaching like this you will find these kinds of activities come very naturally as you move from one musical area to another. Trust your imagination. Spend as little or as long as you like exploring the piece in this way. Challenge pupils gently, always working from their strengths. Reinforce where necessary. Take time to explain carefully if something is not understood. There is no hurry.

The improvisations can be as short or as long as you like: ten seconds or ten minutes! And if you've been using improvisation in one form or another from the first lesson, your pupils will never lack confidence or have any inhibitions when it comes to being creative, playing music by ear or from memory.

The next step is to open the book and explore the piece from notation. With all this careful preparation, the pupil will immediately have some insight, knowledge and understanding. A far cry from stumbling through the piece from bar one.

Improvisation and technique

Here's an example of using improvisation when teaching a technical point. In this case the 'thumb-under' technique for pianists is being introduced for the first time.

The ascending movement of the right hand is described as being like 'the thumb going under a bridge and then the bridge going over the thumb' and the descending movement as 'the bridge going back over the thumb'. Now the pupil is asked to improvise a very slow little piece where the thumb goes under the bridge and the bridge goes back over the thumb twice in each direction. Then the pupil tries the piece again adding a crescendo whenever the music goes higher and a diminuendo when it goes lower. For practice the pupil makes up some more pieces that experiment with thumb movement. The pieces are given titles like *The boat and the bridge* making the movement very smooth; or *Soldiers marching under the bridge*, where the music marches boldly using accents and staccato.

In the next lesson this work would be connected to scales which could be played (improvised) in different characters, colours, smells, tastes, and so on, using a variety of tempi, dynamics, rhythms and articulations based on pieces the pupil is learning or about to learn.

Points to ponder

- Are you comfortable with the idea of improvising or does it worry you? If it does, why?

- When was the last time you improvised?

8 ... and so is composing!

Having found the confidence to improvise, making the step into composition is both short and simple.

When does an improvisation become a composition?

Of course there is no clear-cut answer to this question, but here's a straightforward method for teaching pupils how to turn an improvisation into a composition. Imagine you and your pupils are working on a piece from the tutor which contains the following ingredients:

1	*Title*	An afternoon stroll
2	*Key*	G major
3	*Time signature*	4/4
4	*Tempo marking*	Andante
5	*Markings*	Slurs and ♩, *p* and *f*
6	*Theory*	Melody is based on the interval of a third
7	*Technique*	Control of lyrical legato lines
8	*Character*	Moving gently, relaxed and cheerful

Having identified these ingredients, ask your pupil to make up a title (something similar to the piece in question) and then choose some of the ingredients on which the piece is to be based. Here's an example:

1	*Title*	A walk to the fish and chip shop
2	*Key*	G major (just the first five notes)
3	*Time signature*	4/4
4	*Tempo marking*	Andante
5	*Markings*	Slurs and ♩, *p* and *f*
6	*Character*	Relaxed and cheerful

First of all a little preliminary work to feel at home with the ingredients:
- Feel a 'stroll-like' pulse of 4/4.
- Play the microscale of G major a few times.
- Play the scale *p* and *f*.
- Play the scale incorporating the ♩ marking. Perhaps playing the ascending notes tenuto and descending notes non-tenuto. Or playing alternate notes tenuto/non-tenuto.

Then do a first improvisation of the piece.

Now for some evaluation:
- How well did I match the music to my title?
- Did I use all the ingredients?
- Was there anything I particularly liked?
- How can I improve the piece?

Help pupils to identify little melodic or rhythmic ideas that they liked which could be repeated and form the basis of some structure.

And so to a repeat of the improvisation making changes and refinements as they proceed. Then another evaluation and more refinements.

This kind of work is then taken into the pupil's practice (and indeed becomes a central and recurring practice activity). Perhaps it is further developed and refined over a week (or longer). The improvisation is now becoming a composition. At this stage pupils' writing skills may be well behind their creative skills, but they can still put something on paper using *graphic notation* by drawing marks and shapes to represent the sounds. After a few days' work it may look something like this:

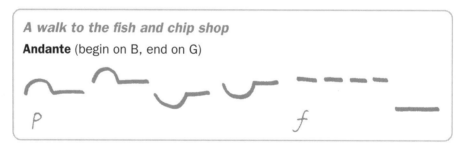

A walk to the fish and chip shop
Andante (begin on B, end on G)

The improvisation has now *become* a composition!

If you teach pupils to combine this kind of graphic notation with their manuscript paper, the result could be even more helpful:

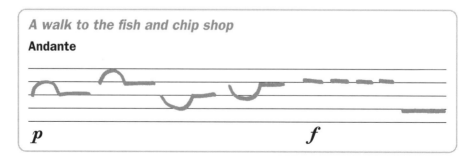

A walk to the fish and chip shop
Andante

Hearing friends or fellow-pupils playing 'your' piece is a terrific motivational boost and this kind of notation is certainly good enough to allow other players to have a go. Perhaps the composer can discuss the performance with the players. How close did it come to the composer's expectation, for example.

If pupils have been learning to write notes and rhythms (and other musical symbols) at each lesson (and practice), then it is probably not going to be a huge leap to arrive at this:

And of course all this work re-connects with the original piece from the tutor on which you and your pupil are working.

Graphic notation can work at even the most rudimentary level. The following could well be possible after just one lesson. Sit at the piano (even if you're not a pianist) and see what you can make of this:

Improvisation, composition and practice

We have already seen that most lessons should ideally begin with aural and musicianship activities, with a good deal of improvisation. Practice should do so too. It is unthreatening, creative and engaging. So, with the ingredients of *An afternoon stroll* in mind, pupils might begin their practice with some work in the key of G major. If they don't know the whole scale, they can certainly work on the microscale of G major with particular emphasis on producing a lovely lyrical legato. They may then make a connection with dynamics and add *p* and *f* to their scale/key practice. Then the scale could be practised playing, for example, every other note with more weight (♩).

Perhaps they might try to improvise a little exercise using the interval of a third. Then more work of their own on *A walk to the fish and chip shop*, refining both the piece and its notation. Then some practice on *An afternoon stroll* itself, perhaps spending some special time on a particularly tricky bit.

Keeping an improvisation diary

Pupils should keep a note of their improvisations in their Musical Passports. If possible they should record the improvisations too, by audio or (preferably) video recording to demonstrate the performance element. Given today's computer technology, many children will find it easy to send these recordings to relatives, friends and possibly even their teacher prior to the lesson.

'I can't compose!'

I've occasionally known pupils (and teachers) who quite categorically announce (and believe) that they *can't* improvise or compose. It may take a little time to develop the necessary confidence, but be assured: we *all* can!

Points to ponder

- When was the last time you composed a piece?
- Compose a little piece or exercise especially for your pupils to play at their next lesson. Notice their response!

9 Making assumptions

[9] But in fact when teaching at any level!

Particularly when teaching beginners,[9] it is very important to avoid making assumptions or, if we do, to be aware that we're making them.

When a pupil does something 'correctly', we may be forgiven for assuming that they've understood it. But it may well be an illusion! Just because they smile and nod their heads when we say 'do you get that?' doesn't necessarily mean that they do. We need to have strategies in place that can guarantee what we've taught *has* been successfully learnt.

> *Successfully learnt* means a pupil can **recognize, understand *and* apply in any situation.**
>
> For example if we are teaching the rhythmic pattern ♩. ♪ we need to be certain our pupil can:
>
> - **Recognize** the pattern as a *dotted crotchet – quaver* rhythm wherever it appears in a bar and whether the tails go up or down.
> - **Understand** 'how it goes' and play it correctly.
> - **Apply** (play) the rhythm in any context: using any notes, with any articulation imposed on the rhythm and in any style of music (for example, as part of a fast dance or a slow expressive movement).

How can we know that they know?

When teaching we need to be aware of what is really going on in our pupils' minds. What are they thinking? What do they see? What do they understand? How are they interpreting what we say?

There are at least four strategies that we can make use of in determining whether successful learning has taken place:
- Teach the same thing in more than one way.
- Ask questions.
- Present the pupils with a task that shows they can apply their understanding.
- Ask pupils to explain to us or teach us what we've taught them.

Teaching the same thing in different ways

Crotchet =
quarter note

Quaver =
eighth note

Virtually everything can be viewed and understood in more than one way and it is important that we use this knowledge when teaching. For example, what do note lengths (crotchets, quavers and so on) tell us? How long a note lasts? Or when to end the note? Or perhaps when to begin the next note? All the possibilities are equally valid. But with which one are you most comfortable? You've probably never thought about it, but whichever one it is will affect the way you teach note lengths. Try teaching the other ways too.

When teaching a new rhythm pattern, for example, always make lots of connections:
- *with aural:* pupils hear the rhythm internally.
- *with memory:* teach pupils to play the rhythm from memory through call-and-response activities.
- *with notation:* teach pupils to play the rhythm from notation.
- *with pulse:* teach pupils how the rhythm relates to the pulse.
- *with theory:* teach pupils to understand the rhythm, e.g. through sub-divisions and the relationship with the pulse.
- *with writing:* teach pupils to write down the rhythm.
- *with improvisation:* ask pupils to improvise using the rhythm.

Teaching the same thing from different angles makes for thoroughness, ensures understanding and can be quite fun too!

Asking questions

I was working with a young violinist recently who was experiencing considerable trouble with notation. She was about to do her Grade One. This was our first meeting and I knew little of her musical ability before we began the session. I prepared this little exercise, in advance, for us to work on:

Minim =
half note

I began by asking her a few questions. She knew the names of the notes and the appropriate strings. She knew about the counting of minims and crotchets. So where was the problem? I needed to find out more about how she was *interpreting* the notation. Here are the exact answers to the questions I put to her:

- What's the difference between the last bar and the first three bars?
  The last bar has got two lines at the end of it.

- Are there any similarities between the first three bars?
  No – they are all different.

- What's the difference between bars one and three?
  Bar one has a **C** *in it.*

[10] Another pupil thought it meant C major.

- What does the **C** mean?
  It's **C** *for 'count'.*[10]

- Are any two bars the same?
  No.

- Is bar one repeated?
  No.

- How many two-beat notes like the first note can you see (including the first note)?
  Four.

- How many minims, like the first note, can you see (including the first note)?
  Four.

- Can you tell me which bars have the high notes?
  Bar two.

These answers spoke volumes and we can learn much from them. By asking questions we can begin to get into the minds of our pupils and begin to see what they are seeing. And what I discovered here was that this student was being hindered in her reading by a number of serious notational misconceptions.

But, having asked these questions, I had to be very careful in my reactions and responses to her answers. Even if answers are not the expected ones, they may still make good sense! Don't assume the expected answer is the only right one. Indeed there is a very good reason for all the answers above! Read them again. And if you're still a little foxed by the final exchange, have a look at the stems of the notes …

What did I assume at the end of this conversation? That this young violinist doesn't 'get' the notation? That her reading will be unreliable and confused? That she's a poor pupil? Clearly a number of concepts needed to be re-considered and it would take some time to do that. But there was an interesting mind at work here. The problem was that her teacher had been making assumptions.

So off we set reconsidering the various issues identified by our conversation and in the process had a lot of fun. It didn't take long to 're-program' this young violinist's perception.

Applying that understanding

To make sure that my young violin pupil had truly absorbed all we had discussed, I had prepared some further exercises which simply used the same ingredients but presented them in a different order. We worked at these for a while and all was well:

Finally, I wrote a couple of exercises that applied the concepts in a different context – this is the crux of understanding:

All was well again and I knew then that the understanding had been absorbed.

Yes, this all takes a little time but not *that* much time and certainly it is time very well worth spending (in both the preparation and execution) as we end up with a pupil who is learning with real understanding. She departed with much more confidence.

Ask pupils to explain to us or teach us what we've taught them

Pupils often enjoy having the tables turned. Ask them to play the part of the teacher and teach us what they've just learned. For example, play something to them from notation with mistakes and see what they are able to correct and how they go about it. Do this regularly and you will learn much.

Other potential assumptions

Actually the list is virtually infinite, but here are a few to get you thinking. When you have a moment, choose one or two and consider the possible implications.

First of all a few elementary concepts that we might assume pupils understand. But do they?

- **High and low or up and down** How do we explain high and low when, for example, the piano goes sideways and you go down the cello when the pitch goes up?
- **Sharp and flat** How many assumptions are we making in thinking pupils will know exactly what being sharp or flat actually means? And there's *being* sharp and flat and notes that are simply called sharps and flats. Is the fact that we say 'F sharp' but it is written 'sharp F' confusing?
- Why is the key signature of C major called a key signature?
- Is 'D' the same as 'D natural'?

We may be making assumptions about what pupils are thinking:
- Are they making the connections as we would wish? (And are they making the connections at all?)
- That they like or dislike a piece.
- Can facial expressions be misleading?

We may be making assumptions about how pupils 'see' music:
- Do they think each *line* of music is in some way significant?
- Do they understand the significance of a key signature?

- Do they understand the significance of tails going up or down?
- Do they know whether accidentals apply to the note they precede or follow? Why do pupils so often forget the rule about maintaining their effect through a bar?

We may be making assumptions about what pupils are doing (or not doing):
- What do we assume if a pupil keeps making the same mistake?
- What assumptions do we make about pupils' practice? How do we deal with these?
- What assumptions might we make if pupils don't practise regularly?
- How do we interpret a lack of response?
- What do we assume if a pupil doesn't seem to be paying attention? Can there be any positive reasons why a pupil's mind wanders?

Points to ponder

- Can you think of any assumptions (perhaps incorrect ones) you may have made about particular pupils?
- Think about something you understand really well and how you developed that understanding.
- How do you know that you understand something?

10 Affirming our musical beliefs

❝ We are the Pilgrims, master; we shall go
Always a little further ... ❞

James Elroy Flecker, Hassan

For all of us in teaching, whatever the length of our experience, it is refreshing, exciting and energising to think about what it is we actually do. It is all too easy to develop habits (good and bad!), sit back or rely on what may have worked before. If we are in the happy position of teaching beginners, it becomes all the more important. We have a huge responsibility to our pupils, so let's consider the broader issues facing the instrumental or singing teacher.

Redefining fun

A fellow music teacher received a letter from a parent saying that her son no longer wanted to 'do exams' but instead simply wanted to 'play for fun'. Feeling that the teacher would be neither interested in teaching her son for fun, nor know how to do so, she requested the termination of lessons.

There does indeed seem to be a belief that pupils either 'do exams' or 'play for fun'. Some teachers say things like 'It's nearly the end of the lesson, let's play a piece for fun,' or, 'now that we've done the exam let's play for fun for a while', or 'try to play something for fun during your practice'. All this talk of fun builds up a false impression about the things we do.

By labelling certain pieces or activities as fun simply strengthens the belief that the other pieces and activities are not! And what is the opposite of having fun? Most dictionaries will tell you that it's being *bored*. Boredom comes from a lack of involvement and imagination. Imaginative teaching can make anything fun and Simultaneous Learning is designed to keep both teachers and pupils involved, stimulated and indeed having fun, however serious the matter in hand. This kind of thorough teaching removes obstacles to learning and hugely reduces the potential for making mistakes, creating a stress-free atmosphere for teaching and learning. Let's avoid the fun problem by making everything fun. Even learning scales can be fun, when approached with imagination!

Think back to your own favourite teachers. What do they have in common? Almost certainly it is that they presented their subjects with a great deal of fun, which was probably the result of their thoroughly connected approach (as well as their sense of humour!).

Dealing with practical problems

I had some of my first lessons in a cupboard. It was quite a large cupboard, but a cupboard nevertheless. But I remember those lessons as being highly engaging and enjoyable because my teacher was focused, had a good sense of humour and was himself clearly not fazed at all by the surroundings. I always thought it rather fun being taught in a cupboard. It is highly unlikely that we'll ever find ourselves teaching in a cupboard these days, but we may sometimes get frustrated with our teaching conditions. If you teach in a school, it may be that you find yourself put in a less than suitable room or perhaps the heating may have broken down. Do your best not to be fazed under such circumstances. On the whole, pupils don't mind where they are taught. They probably won't mind about the temperature either. But they might mind if we mind, if we become grumpy and our teaching suffers as a result. Whatever difficulties or frustrations (large or small) we may have, always leave them outside the teaching room.

I know this great short cut ...

Beware of short cuts and quick fixes, they almost always ultimately fail, as pupils don't really understand what it is they are doing. Teaching only part of the picture, for example: knowing a piece, but not knowing what key it's in; not being able to play the related scale, or not knowing what character the piece is trying to convey or not even knowing what the title is (or what it means). Only knowing vaguely 'how a rhythm goes' but not really understanding it. Not understanding the principles of fingering because the teacher always marks it in. Or not being able to read pieces at roughly the same level as those being learnt.

I recall a teacher who had a pupil who was very poor rhythmically. Rather than going back to basics and working it out, step-by-step, they concocted an extraordinary hit-and-miss method (this note lasts about a second, this one's *really* long, this one's as short as you can play it ...). It worked (very approximately) for one or two simple pieces but naturally the pupil soon gave up in a state of complete disarray. We all know short cuts and certain teachers are masters of the quick fix. Occasionally in our enthusiasm to get beginners moving on, we may be tempted to throw in the odd short cut. But if our principles are sound and Simultaneous Learning thorough, potential short cuts become unnecessary. They don't do our pupils any good in the long run.

But my pupil simply won't count ...

There is a story of a teaching diploma examination where the teacher-candidate was asked what he'd do if the pupil simply 'won't count'. 'Keep on telling him to' was the confident answer! If we use Simultaneous Learning, then each time we have to remind pupils we can make further connections; we can teach the same thing from different perspectives. Frustrations (both ours and that of our pupils) should become a thing of the past!

There are a number of reasons why pupils get things wrong:

- They simply don't understand (and they probably haven't made the right connections) so …
- They forget because they didn't understand.
- They may be lazy (or careless)!

As long as pupils do their best to learn from their mistakes, there is no shame in getting things wrong. If, on the other hand, pupils really persist in getting the same things wrong again and again, then clearly there is a deeper problem. Take some time to find out more and explore this with them. Progress will not take place if there are major psychological obstructions in the way. Remember that simply correcting a mistake is not teaching.

Helpful parents

If possible, encourage parents to sit in on lessons from time to time. (The Suzuki method relies on huge parental involvement; parents also learn to play the instrument, which allows them to take a real part in the learning and practice process.) Talk to parents about the musical relationship at home so that practice occupies a special place in family life and time is set aside to listen to performances of pieces, exercises, even scales. It is very important that children don't feel musically isolated in the family environment: this can seriously limit motivation and progress.

So where *are* we going?

Our ultimate goal is to provide our pupils with the finest of gifts, the means of making music musically. In teaching beginners we are, as it were, embarking on a search for a holy grail, developing a *process* which will allow our pupils, with albeit varying degrees of expertise, to enjoy the great gift of independent music-making.

The *process* of this grail pursuit is crucially important. Indeed, it is the all-important factor. We must never let the thought of the *outcome* overshadow the *process*. However attractive that outcome – passing an instrumental or singing exam, a diploma with honours, or an international career – it is the process which really matters, the search for the holy grail, all the way through from its most important early stages.

Teachers are often working hard and pushing pupils vigorously forward but with little ultimate reward because it may not be the right direction for the pupil. It's as if we are running fast to get somewhere, but we never actually get there because we're running in the wrong direction!

So what do we do next? What will drive our teaching forward after the first lessons, described above? Will we rely on the exam system to instil a single-minded desire to compel our pupils to jump through ever-more-daunting musical hoops, until, at some point, they give up, the joy of music making having disappeared somewhere along the way? Or will we be process-driven rather than outcome-driven, aware of the virtues of Simultaneous Learning where we offer something more, something infinitely richer: a zeal to establish a hugely enjoyable and rewarding process, as our pupils take their first eager steps towards the acquisition of a precious gift which could last them a lifetime?

> The answer is that we simply continue teaching our pupils to be musicians. The Four Ps provide the values and framework on which we hang our teaching with Simultaneous Learning providing the method.

Creating your own teaching programme

As you plan and develop this all-important process for your eager new pupils, have the confidence to create your own teaching programme. It really is quite simple. And because it's your own programme you will feel so much more motivated to teach it with real enthusiasm. Once you get into this kind of thinking it will become second nature. Our pupils will be receiving a much more wide-ranging, all-embracing kind of musical education. It is a very exciting prospect.

Here's how to create your own teaching programme:

- Teach the Simultaneous Learning way *through lots of repertoire*, always making connections as you go along.
- Explore different genres and styles of music.
- Set pupils little projects.
- Try to give pupils as many performing opportunities as possible.
- Ensure that everything is being learnt thoroughly.
- Encourage pupils to build up and shape their own personal musical ID by regularly updating their Musical Passports.

By all means drop in for an exam from time to time, but only when it would represent a completely positive experience. Pupils' abilities should be, at the very least, equal to (or ideally ahead) of the exam in question. With Simultaneous Learning techniques, pupils should be able to deal with all sections of a music exam confidently and comfortably, finding it a stress-free and enjoyable experience.

Be positive

In today's troubled world, where statistics and league tables are often mistaken for educational excellence, many young people are put under enormous and quite unnecessary stress, forever doing tests, receiving criticism and undergoing assessment. Don't let your music teaching add to the general mayhem! Instead, let's always teach *positively*, allowing all pupils to shine in their own particular way. By the end of the first term they may have learnt to play a Mozart minuet or they may have learnt to improvise on two notes. Either is fine.

Moving forward ... breaking free

Ideas about teaching are always evolving and moving forward. Some of us, however, find it uncomfortable to move with them. We feel we are being forced out of our comfort zones into unknown regions – into new and strange waters. But adjusting, and even changing our ideas becomes easy if we have strong core values which remain unchanged and represent the heart of our musical personalities. It is really only the way we present these core values that changes. And that's much less daunting.

I hope you feel the values that have been explored in this book – the Four Ps and the various supplementary principles – agree wholly with your own. These fundamental musical values never change. What I hope to have suggested here are new ways to deliver those values. The Simultaneous Learning process is probably only an extension of what you do already. So it should be relatively easy to develop, to try out new strategies, to be a proactive teacher. Our fundamental musical personalities remain unchanged. Confidence in moving forward should strengthen as we become more accustomed to these ideas.

Tales of the unexpected

I always enjoy books that don't quite end as we might expect. So here's a little twist in the tale ...

We have looked in depth at teaching beginners. But in fact all these strategies and ideas can be applied to teaching at any level – from beginner to post-graduate, whatever the ambitions of our pupils may be. So we come full circle. In chapter one we considered the qualities of the best students on the point of graduating from a music conservatoire. We have seen that the principles which support teaching those students are exactly the same as those guiding our beginners. All effective teachers belong to the same alliance. We have one common aspiration.

So good luck and enjoy your teaching – there are very few professions that can be more rewarding.

Coda: 'Them' on us!

I thought the pupils might have the last word!

What do you remember about your first lesson?

'I remember sitting in my primary school staff room with around a dozen other seven or eight-year-olds, clapping rhythms with the violin teacher. I remember thinking the teacher was the tallest man I'd ever seen – and I was mesmerised by his long pony-tail! My ability to repeat his rhythms meant I was lucky enough to be one of the 'chosen few' to have individual lessons with him.'

'I was told to pretend the reed was my favourite type of ice cream. As a precocious so-and-so I said my favourite type was caramel.'

'I can remember nothing of the content of my lessons, other than that my clarinet case smelt funny (the instrument was borrowed from the school's stock and had clearly seen better days). My teacher was fairly serious, though all I can remember of him was his awful taste in ties and a Bobby-Charlton-like comb-over!'

'I remember my first lesson clearly. My violin teacher was a real character, ex-army and probably a brass player rather than a string player! He had a moustache, smoked a pipe and gave me a lacrosse stick. I don't remember much about him as a teacher, but he made the lessons fun and took an interest in all three of us in the group.'

'My teacher was incredibly enthusiastic and energetic about music and teaching, and lessons were always inspiring.'

'… A very bashed-up horn and Tune a Day …'

What kind of pupil were you at the start?

'Clueless but punctual!' 'Confident but wayward.' 'Very, very shy.' 'Precocious – little know-it-all-brat!' 'Shy and overwhelmed by my teacher …'

'The little old lady up the road had absolutely no idea that I was playing everything from memory and by ear … Very slow progress but I didn't notice or mind.'

'I was always asking questions and was frustrated with myself for not being able to do everything perfectly first time.'

'I remember looking forward to my lessons and being very excited.'

Can you remember any qualities of your first teacher?

'He explained things very clearly, was always very perceptive of everything I did. He had a terrific sense of humour, but a fiery temper too! I rarely got past the first ten bars as he would always stop me as soon as one thing went wrong, so I hardly ever played a piece the whole way through.'

'A boring, inflexible dragon. I felt humiliated and bullied – it was very negative.'

'She arrived in a sports car and was dynamic! A very good player who was inspirational, and we laughed a lot too. I was lucky to have her. A great teacher can affect your outlook on life.'

'He gave me handwritten studies designed just for me each week – excellent exercises I still use today! He would go along with whatever whim I had that day and make progress with it.'

'As I got older, I began to appreciate something quite special about my piano teacher. He had always made sure that theory and aural was part of the lesson – it was never seen as a side-issue or something to loathe (as some of my peers did). It also meant that when it came to exams, the aural tests came much more naturally and were nothing to be afraid of.'

'He was trying to keep one page ahead of me in Tune a Day !'

'Inspiring – he would go off in many different directions – much where his imagination took him.'

'He was very arrogant and thought his views were correct without listening to others.'

'She seemed to want to teach me.'

'He had an incredible energy and enthusiasm for the music, which always came across. It was definitely music first and technique second, which was good in many ways, as lessons were always musically rewarding and interesting.'

Did you practise?

'My teacher was very good at being scary and ensuring I practised … I had to keep a log for the piano – I frequently fabricated the amount of time spent.'

'Not enough. That which I did was out of duty, though my relationship with my clarinet was soured by the odd smell ...'

'My parents would rather I didn't! We had a practise notebook issued by the school – I lied every week. Consequently I became good at sight-reading.'

'I shared a quarter-size cello so practice was quite a sociable event. I practised at school with the other girl who shared the cello and took it home alternate weekends.'

'Absolutely. Primarily because I was always keen to be able to do more and was interested in how it worked. But also out of love for performing and respect for my teacher.'

'75% down to wanting to learn and to please my teacher, and 25% down to fairly potent parental pressure.'

'I was always confused by my dad saying, "Don't play it until you can play it properly"!'

Also by Paul Harris

Improve your teaching!

Encouraging and inspirational, this is a 'must have' handbook for all instrumental and singing teachers. Outlining Paul Harris' innovative strategy of 'Simultaneous Learning' and packed with comprehensive advice and practical strategies, it offers creative and accessible solutions to the challenges faced in music education.

Improve your practice!

This series encourages students to plan their practice sessions, starting with warm-ups and then giving tips on how to 'explore a piece'. These books enable children to think about different aspects of music as they practise, giving them a better understanding of their pieces and encouraging independent thought and exploration.

Improve your aural!

Designed to take the fear out of aural through fun listening activities, boxes to fill in and practice exercises, these workbooks, each with CD, focus on all the elements of the aural test. A range of interconnected activities are included to help develop the ear, including singing, clapping, playing your instrument, writing music down, improvising and composing. Fulfils all ABRSM exam requirements.

Improve your sight-reading!

This series of workbooks is designed to help overcome sight-reading problems, especially in the context of graded examinations. Step by step players build up a complete picture of each piece, first through rhythmic and melodic exercises, then by the study of prepared pieces with associated questions for the student to answer, and finally to a series of practice tests.

Improve your scales!

Using 'finger fitness' exercises, scale and arpeggio study pieces and simple improvisations, Paul Harris' brilliant method teaches students to know the notes and thus to play scales and arpeggios with real confidence. Forms a solid basis for the learning of repertoire and sight-reading techniques, as well as being invaluable preparation for exams.

For more information go to Paulharrismusic.com